TABLE OF CONTENTS

TRADITIONAL
Here's a Bunch of Flowers For You 13
In A Silver Bowl 14
Hats Off For A Garden Party 16
Putting On The Ritz 17
The All Green Centerpiece 21
You Did It! 23

UNUSUAL
Celebrating For The Twenty-Fifth Time 24
Capture A Rainbow 26
Invite A Rabbit To Your Party 27
Boxes And Boxes And Boxes 28
Shower Tower 30
Displaying Your Collectibles 31

GLASS
Through A Glass Bowl, Clearly 32
Winter Is Ice And Glass 34
Let Them Float 35
Permanent Summer Centerpiece 36
A Fountain Of Foliage 37

JAPANESE
Lady In The Garden 39
Create A Water Scene 40
Only Three Flowers For Each Table 41

POTTED PLANTS
Use Your House Plants 43
Graduation Celebration 45
A Basket Of Spring 46

A GIFT OF FLOWERS
A Small Gift 47
A Gift From The Sea 48
Make Them Ahead 49

DRIED AND ARTIFICIAL
A Centerpiece of Silk and Dried Materials 51
Silk Flowers For Apartment Dwellers 53

HOLIDAYS
Thanksgiving 55
Christmas Holly and Lights 56
Create A Christmas Scene 57
A Christmas Tree Centerpiece 59
Make Your Own Christmas Candle 61
A Bowl of Christmas Balls 63
Try These Fancy Easter Eggs 65

WEDDING
The Wedding Rehearsal Dinner 66
Poinsettias For A Winter Wedding 67

When The Reception Tables Are
  Long and Narrow   69
Let The Good Luck Rice Be Your
  Centerpiece   71
LUNCHEON AND BANQUET TABLES
Wine Bottles A Go-Go   73
Paper Bag Containers   75
Flowers and Records For A Musical
  Occasion   77

Get Some Help From The Magazines   79
The Old Fan In The Clay Pot Trick   80
Baskets and Bows   81
For A Card Party   83
Make It Big With Yarn-Wrapped Cans   85
A Table of Suggestions For Inexpensive
  Centerpiece Designs   86

Jean Hallstead's

BOOK OF CENTERPIECES

Illustrated by
Ellen Parsons

Prospect Hill
Baltimore, Maryland

Dedicated to my maternal grandmother who planted the seed that became a lifelong love of flowers and to my husband who has been an inspiration and always there with an encouraging word.

BOOK OF CENTERPIECES

Copyright © 1986 by Jean Hallstead
All rights reserved
Library of Congress Catalog Card #86-62811
ISBN 0-941526-03-8
Published by Prospect Hill
216 Wendover Road
Baltimore, Maryland 21218

Over the years as more and more friends have asked me for help with planning table arrangements for everything from having a few friends in for dinner to large public banquets, it has become clear that something that is easy and fun for me is difficult for many people. The hardest of all, it seems, are centerpieces. People are afraid they might be working against some mysterious code of unbreakable rules—from this school or that course—which intimidates more than helps them.

But rules are no more than guidelines to make things simple and easy. I hope this book will help you go beyond rules and free your inhibitions. Use your imagination! Look for the unusual.

I get a lot of telephone calls asking for last-minute advice about creating party centerpieces. The luncheon is next week and the group has been saving tuna cans. Now what?

Thinking about the table decorations should be done early in the planning stages for any event. Organize your thoughts. Decide what you are going to do, and do it. Check centerpieces off your worry list.

Here are some simple guidelines for planning.

1. What is the budget? Can you buy everything, or will you have to use tuna cans and garden flowers?
2. How many arrangements will be needed? Will there be a head table? All the centerpieces should be alike, but the design at the head table should be larger.
3. How large are the tables? Is the decor colonial, modern, oriental, or rustic? The centerpieces should suit the room

and the tables for which they are designed.

4. Is there a theme? Certain occasions seem to call for white, others say red. I tend to think of pink many times, because pink is such a happy color. Baskets say spring to me. Would a little glitter be appropriate? Inexpensive oriental objects, such as fans and paper lanterns, can sometimes convey a message. This is the fun part of planning.

Winter is the hardest time of the year for fresh plant material. At any other time, you can get material from gardens or roadsides, but not during winter. Then you really have to think about how to keep the cost down. It is a good time of the year for combining house plant leaves with bare branches and colorful tablecloths. Anything is possible, if you give it some thought.

Color is not too worrisome. In nature all the colors mingle together happily. I worry about color only if someone else feels strongly about it, or if the room has one strong color that has to be accommodated.

Think ahead. That is the secret. You should have a very good idea of what you are going to do before you buy your first flower or cut your first leaf. For any truly special occasion, always make a sample centerpiece ahead of time to make sure it is what you want and that your idea really works.

Originally this book was planned to progress from simple table arrangements for your own family, through private dinner parties, to more elaborate parties, and on to large public parties with many tables to be decorated. However, a good friend, reading through the book for me, suggested it would be more helpful if all similar centerpieces were together. In a cookbook, she said, the meat recipes are together and the desserts are together. It makes it easier to browse, she said. The reader knows if she wants to prepare for two or twenty.

So within this book you will find similar designs placed together. I hope you will browse, and that it will lead you to discover that, indeed, there are no rules here; only suggestions. A centerpiece that you enjoy making for your own dining room table may also be the very thing for the church supper with twenty tables to decorate. Mix and match, add and subtract, trim leaves, insert wires, glue together, break apart, keep it simple, or pull out all the stops. Go beyond rules.

Most arrangements start with their containers. The purpose of the container is to hold the decorative material and to be a part of the overall design. Usually a bowl, basket or tray, a container can actually be anything you find attractive that will do the job.

The mechanics of centerpieces are the hidden support systems of the designs. I will be suggesting *pinholders,* which are heavy metal objects that look like upturned needles onto which you impale flower and foliage stems; *cup pinholders,* which are pinholders built into heavy metal containers that hold water; *green floral foam,* a plastic material for supporting stems that will hold water if it is submerged for a short time, *brown floral foam,* similar to green floral foam but it does not hold water and will sup-

port heavier dried and wire stems; and *styrofoam,* a stiff white or green plastic foam, which is used as a base for several centerpiece ideas. Plastic foam materials usually need to be held in a container by crossing two lengths of plastic adhesive *green floral tape* over the top of the foam and down over the container. *Waxy floral tape,* sticky on both sides, is a paper tape used to wrap around stems, paddings, wires, and even flowers, to hold them together and disguise contrivances. It is available in several colors. Pinholders may be held in place in the bottom of containers with *green floral clay.* The clay is pinched off, rubbed between the palms to form long rolls of clay, and the rolls are placed around the outside edges of the bottom of the pinholder. The clay may be difficult to remove, however, so be cautious about using it on really fine porcelain and silver containers. Pinholders and cup pinholders are expensive, so the foam is used when centerpieces travel from home. All of the suggested mechanics are available at florist shops and garden centers.

Flowers and foliage are the prime ingredients of centerpieces because they are beautiful and ephemeral. However, you don't want them so ephemeral that they don't last through a party, so always prepare them for use by soaking them in water. Flower arrangers call this conditioning the plant material. Foliage should be completely immersed for at least an hour before use. Flowers are placed in deep containers up to their heads for the same time. Soaking overnight is not too long for either flowers or foliage. Avoid placing dried plant materials in water.

Features in centerpieces are alternative or additional to plant material. Anything from playing cards on sticks to jewelry can be used, and used to advantage.

Bases can be trays, mats, mirrors, slices of wood, or scatterings of seeds or sea shells. Their purpose is to enhance the centerpiece by tying together all of its parts or by enlarging the overall effect.

A very useful aid when creating centerpiece designs is *floral spray paint.* It comes in a wide assortment of colors, it is waterproof, it dries quickly, it will not disintegrate styrofoam as most paints do, and it can be used on metal, paper, plastic, and plant material alike.

Less than half of the designs photographed for this book were done by myself. During the time the book was in progress, several friends agreed to test the clarity of my directions by trying to follow them—with results so pleasing that their designs were photographed and used for the book instead of mine. Thank you Ann, Cardy, Ellen and Ellie.

I hope that the pages which follow will be of help in your own creative efforts and that they stimulate your imagination, becoming a springboard for artistic accomplishment beyond the ideas and suggestions offered in this book.

Vases with narrow necks come in many colors, styles, and sizes.

HERE'S A BUNCH OF FLOWERS FOR YOU!

Here is the classic flower arranger's dilemma. You are presented with a handful of florist flowers by a thoughtful arriving guest. The bunch contains flowers of assorted sizes and colors. They need to go into water immediately and you have limited time to arrange them.

The solution rests with the container. Let a narrow-neck container do the job for you. Simply grasp the bunch of flowers in one hand at approximately the place where they will hit the container's neck and shuffle the flowers and stems around and up and down until the effect is pleasing. Then hold the bunched flowers up to the neck of the container, already filled with water, and cut off the stems so they will rest evenly on the bottom of the container. When the stems are in the water, the neck of the container should hold them together just as your hand did!

To co-ordinate colors, tie a pretty scarf or ribbon around the container.

IN A SILVER BOWL

For that special dinner party, nothing quite outshines a centerpiece of flowers in a silver bowl. If you use silver often, spray-paint a large, three-inch pinholder with silver paint so it will be less likely to show through your flowers. Be sure to coat the bottom of any pinholder you place in silver with clear lacquer so there will be no rust deposits on your bowl.

When working in silver, or any valuable container, do not risk using sticky floral tape or clay, which may be difficult to remove. If you are afraid the holder will slip, just fold a piece of damp newspaper into a pad and place it under the pinholder.

Silver bowls come in many shapes and sizes, but the design described here is adaptable for almost any of them. If your table is oblong or rectangular instead of round or square, you may prefer a long, narrow centerpiece. This can be accomplished by altering the length of the "boundary" flowers—the first flowers placed.

Because of the size of this arrangement, the flowers should be tall, but they need not

be crowded. Keep it light and airy. There is nothing worse than a centerpiece that keeps conversation from flowing across the dinner table.

You will need at least fifteen large flowers, such as daffodils, tulips, chrysanthemums, carnations, or zinnias. Select flowers that will have an impact. If your bowl is large, more flowers will be needed. You will need the same number of foliage stems as there are flowers.

Place the tallest flower, which should be about eighteen inches tall, in the very center of your pinholder. Next place four flowers evenly around the outside edge of the bowl, dividing the bowl into quarters. They should be placed almost parallel to the surface of the table, and if you are working in a round bowl and want to create a round design, all of them should be the same length, about twelve inches. These first five flowers are your boundaries. None of the remaining material should be longer. Now is the time to alter the shape of your centerpiece. If you want an oblong design, two of the opposing flowers should be shorter, about eight inches long.

Next place five stems of foliage in the area between the flowers. Ferns are especially good for this, or you might use house plant leaves. Herb foliage is marvelous.

Fill in with more flowers all around. More foliage can be added. Try to make the arrangement even on all sides. Check for flat areas. The pinholder should be obscured from view by the foliage.

Gray-tone foliage such as artemesia, rue, santolina, or Atlantic cedar is especially pretty in silver. In fact, an all green arrangement is really spectacular in silver.

HATS OFF FOR A GARDEN PARTY

For a festive out-of-doors party, or a wedding in the garden, consider using an inverted large-brimmed straw hat as the container for each centerpiece. Place an empty margarine tub, which has been filled with floral foam, inside the crown of each hat.

Use only yellow and white daisies to give the occasion a feeling of charm and gaiety. Twelve stems of flowers and eighteen stems of assorted ferns will be needed for each hat. Arrange the flowers so they are loose and flowing with some of them leaning outward over the brim, as opposed to having them all stick up straight from the crown. For a further touch of color, tie a band of ribbon around the bowl of each floppy straw hat, allowing long streamers to flow from the bows.

Make the arrangements the afternoon of the day before the party and keep them in a cool, dark place such as the garage or basement until they are needed.

PUTTING ON THE RITZ

When keeping it simple is not your intention, and you want a really lavish centerpiece with an abundance of flowers, you will be creating what flower arrangers call a mass arrangement. This kind of centerpiece is not difficult, but it can be expensive if you have to buy the plant material. The following list is a minimum of what will be needed. More flowers can always be used. Make sure you have at least:

18 tall, spiky flowers such as snapdragons, delphiniums, or celosia

21 chrysanthemums or daisy-like flowers

8 large, showy flowers such as tulips, roses, iris

24 small flowers, such as sweet peas, mini-carnations, or Peruvian lilies

A bunch of filler flowers such as baby's breath or statice

Foliage—at least twelve stems of fern if you are buying. If you are gathering from a garden, use herbs, grasses, branches from shrubs just emerging from winter with their leaves just peeking—no heavy foliage. You will also need several sprigs of ivy or philodendron.

If the arrangement is to be used as a centerpiece for a dining table, the stem length of flowers and foliage should not be so long that the finished design will be too high for conversation to take place over it. If, on the other hand, your mass arrangement is to be placed on a side or buffet table, the tallest flower (the first flower you will place and, ultimately, the uppermost point in the design) should be at least one and one half times the height plus the width of the container. Taller is even better.

When the flowers you are using come in sprays, take the stems apart keeping the individual flower stems as long as possible. Chrysanthemums, for instance, frequently have eight or nine flowers on a spray.

Since an arrangement like this looks better if it is slightly raised, the ideal container would be a large footed compote. A low bowl should be placed on a stand. Support for your arrangement could be provided by an extra large pinholder fixed to the bottom of your container with floral clay, but it is easier to use a large brick of dampened green floral foam held in your container with two crossed lengths of floral tape. However, CAUTION, do not use tape over filigree or gold trim because the gold may come off with the tape. Floral clay may be difficult to remove from the bottom of a really fine container.

Begin making this arrangement by placing the tallest of the spiky flowers in the center of the container, standing upright. This will be the highest point in your completed design. Make sure it is the correct height for your purpose. Now place the next four spiky flowers at equal distances around the outside edges of your arrangement. Insert the stems into the foam so they are parallel with the surface of the table just above the container. Or, if you are using a pinholder, push the sides of the stems onto the points.

If you want your completed arrangement to be more oval than round, make the side flowers longer than the front and back flowers. These first five flowers are the boundaries for the entire design so make sure they are long enough. Except for a little ivy or philodendron cascading over the edge of the container, you will not go beyond them.

Now insert five stems of foliage evenly throughout the arrangement, always staying within the boundaries set by the first five flowers.

Place the remaining tall spiky flowers, followed by an equal number of greens.

Add the chrysanthemums. Try to get them spaced evenly throughout.

Next, place the eight large flowers.

Now add the filler material—baby's breath, statice, or both, and the remaining foliage—working to complete the fullness of the arrangement. Check for any holes in the design.

The last flowers to go in are the small ones. This is your final chance to balance color and fullness. As a finishing touch, place sprigs of ivy or philodendron to cascade over the edge of the container.

This late summer mass arrangement has only zinnias, marigolds, and golden celosia flowers. The celosia serves for both spiky flowers and filler flowers.

A tall aspidistra leaf from a houseplant is the important leaf with two stems of red-tipped photinia and aucuba sprays from two different garden plants growing underneath.

THE ALL GREEN CENTERPIECE

To create a refreshing, light and airy, all-green centerpiece, begin by gathering an assortment of foliage from your garden or the florist shop. Choose different shapes and colors. It is the combination of leaves that will be interesting. Use some house plant foliage.

There should be at least one important leaf—a multi-colored caladium, a split-leaf philodendron, or a large variegated hosta leaf, for instance. Gray-tone artemesia or dusty miller, russet-colored ajuga, stems of tiny-leafed herbs, or an unfurling fern frond will all add their own charm. Because leaves, like flowers, should be conditioned so they will remain fresh in your centerpiece, submerge them completely for at least an hour in deep water before you begin to arrange them.

Choose a long, low container, long enough so the water will show. There is nothing more refreshing than water. Place a pinholder in the center of the container. The color of the pinholder should match the container as much as possible.

Start with the tallest, most important leaf. Everything else should be made to look as if it were growing under it. Next, cover the pinholder. Parsley is good for this. Whatever is used should be low and moss-like. Then simply place the remaining foliage in the pinholder so it looks as if it were growing there. You should be able to see individual leaves. Try for an overall effect of natural growth. A small ceramic turtle or fish could be placed in the water.

One of the exploding balls is a cat toy. The others were made from three by five-inch file cards, cut into narrow strips and taped together. One is natural, the other spray-painted blue.

YOU DID IT!

You got the job! You won the lottery! Congratulations on your first new car! It's a personal triumph occasion that calls for a celebration. The centerpiece should explode with joy.

Begin with an eighteen-inch royal blue or black tray, either square or oval, in the center of the table. To give the effect of an explosion or fireworks, buy or fabricate six or seven open-work balls. They are available, ready-made, from pet stores where they are sold as cat toys. Usually they have little bells inside to amuse or confound the cat. Something similar can be made by fitting two circles—such as come inside roles of tape—inside one another. You could make your own circles out of cardboard strips. Make your balls in assorted sizes. Keep them white, or spray them with floral paint.

Red, white, and blue flowers for the centerpiece will be placed in a large black cup pinholder. You will need:

Three 24-inch white gladiola stems. Snap off the top few buds that will never bloom.

Three 18-inch round red flowers—tulips, roses, or poppies.

Three 12-inch large blue flowers—iris or delphinium—or six or seven bachelor's buttons.

Five large green leaves—hosta or aspidistra.

Begin by placing the tallest flower and work your way down and around. You may want to wire several of the decorative balls onto wire stems and add them to the flower arrangement.

CELEBRATING FOR THE TWENTY-FIFTH TIME!

Or Any Important Occasion

This highly stylized centerpiece will really add some razzle-dazzle to a Twenty-fifth Wedding Anniversary party. The design calls for a trio of containers to be used together, but it would be possible to use only one of them.

Begin with three similar containers of different heights. Ideal, if you have them, would be three tall, mirrored box containers—twelve, nine, and six inches tall. Talk about special! But they could be hard to find. Any three tall containers of a similar shape and color will work. Fill each container with wads of paper or packing "peanuts" so the stems of the design material will not have to reach to the bottom, then place a pinholder on the top. Wedge the pinholder in place firmly with the wadding material so it will not shift. The containers should be filled with water.

Each container will need an interesting, tall, twisted branch, painted white, for its main stem. The branches and other plant material should decrease in size with each container. Frequently such branches can be purchased from a florist. If you do not have access to twisted branches, or the time to search them out, a similar effect can be created with wire. Simply twist a length of medium-weight florist wire around a large can, being careful to allow enough wire for a stem. Remove the can and spray the twisted wire with white gloss paint. A piece of tubing, a plastic straw, or a length of reed will be needed to help hold the wire onto the pinholder.

For foliage, use some kind of bold tropical leaves such as ti, a large philodendron, ginger, bird of paradise, or any large, interesting leaves from your own houseplants. Place several leaves in each arrangement, manipulated so they fit in and around twists in the main stem.

The flowers will be orchids—the big exotic white or purple corsage variety. Since orchid flowers usually have short stems, a wad of wet cotton should be taped to the end of each flower. Twist wire around the taped cotton and use the wire ends to fix the flowers into the arrangement wherever they are most effective. Experiment by holding them in several places until you discover the best locations. Try to make them look as if they were growing from the main white branch. The large arrangement could take three flowers. Two flowers would be needed for the medium-sized design, and one for the smallest. The flowers should all face in different directions. A substitute flower might be protea.

When you are wiring the flowers onto the branches, you may add a few wire tendrils. Make them by coiling wire around a pencil. The wire should be either painted white or wrapped in white floral tape. Pull out the pencil and the wire remains coiled like a vine tendril.

The medium-size design in a nine-inch pillar container is shown in the photograph. There are two branches, two leaves, and two flowers. The leaves should be like two hands embracing the flowers.

CAPTURE A RAINBOW

Look in toy stores or catalogs for a set of bright, colorful, clear plastic notched discs or squares that can be fitted together to form interesting constructions. With these discs build two separate structures, each about eight to ten inches tall.

For a base, place two 12-inch square mirror tiles, available from building supply houses, one angled across the other to make an eight point star. Put the two colorful constructions in the center of the mirrors. Place a small cup pinholder inside each of the constructions and insert a few shiny round leaves in each holder.

The centerpiece is just as effective with no foliage at all. Small stuffed animals peeking out of the shimmering toy castles would create a whimsical centerpiece for a children's birthday party.

INVITE A RABBIT TO YOUR PARTY

A favorite stuffed animal makes an endearing centerpiece. The beloved bear or bunny should stand upright and be about twelve inches tall.

For Easter, a rabbit could wear a quickly-cut calico apron with a few paint brushes inserted at a rakish angle and a basket of painted Easter eggs at his side. A few more painted eggs could surround his feet.

For a birthday party, a stuffed animal could stand beside a basket containing a small plant. Or, a bouquet of flowers in a jar of water could be placed in the basket with the jar concealed by cellophane Easter grass. In either case, foliage can fill in empty spaces.

BOXES AND BOXES AND BOXES

If you collect boxes of any kind, such as cigar boxes, old-fashioned tin cracker boxes, or carved jewelry boxes, you can use them to create fascinating table displays. Even one interesting box can become the feature of a centerpiece.

Simply place a low container of water inside the box and put your flowers and foliage in the container. If the water container has a wide opening, a piece of dampened green floral foam could be taped inside. Flowers should be placed in descending order from the back to the front of the arrangement. There should be enough plant material to completely obscure the mechanics. Non-perishable decorative material such as feathers, dried or silk flowers, sea shells, or jewelry should be similarly arranged.

Your centerpiece could be a collection of boxes. All of them could contain flowers, or only one box need be filled with flowers. It's your house, do it your way. There are no hard and fast rules in your own home. Spill ribbons out of the boxes. Have a fan propped up in one of the boxes. Variations are limited only by your imagination.

One bunch of flowers from your garden or a florist's "bunch of the week," and a few sprays of Baker's fern should do the job. If you have house plants, use your own foliage, especially fern because it replaces its leaves so quickly. Ivy, philodendron, or pothos could be used. The foliage might even form roots in the container!

Or, just put a house plant into one of the boxes. Cover the edges of the box with moss. Excelsior would be effective if you are using a wooden box.

A pretty open box with jewelry spilling out of it can be lovely as a centerpiece. First fill the box with tissue paper and lay the jewelry over that. Short sprigs of green may be stuck in the box. Large single beads may be added where needed, by fixing them to a wire. Just wrap a little sticky green floral tape around the top of the wire, and push the bead down over the tape so it won't drop. That way you will be able to get the bead off the wire when you dismantle the center-piece, and you can use it again.

The jewelry-in-the-box trick can be worked with three boxes all facing in different directions. If more than one box is used, they should be similar in style or period.

This design, intended for a week-long display, uses no fresh material at all. Peacock feathers, sea shells glued on sticks, dried straw flowers, a fan, and a string of beads will look as fresh on the last day as they do on the first.

SHOWER TOWER

Why not make the gaily-wrapped shower gifts themselves the featured centerpiece at your next shower? Whether it's a bridal or welcome-the-new-baby shower, gifts are usually wrapped with careful attention to the occasion. Their featured appearance as a centerpiece would honor both the giver and the receiver.

Just leave the center of the table empty and pile the gifts together as they arrive. Bouquets of silk flowers or a bright oriental paper umbrella could top the pile, if you think it needs further embellishment.

DISPLAYING YOUR COLLECTIBLES

Collections can form the basis for wonderful centerpieces. Coins, shells, rocks, ceramic birds, or whatever you collect can be displayed in the center of a table on trays, on mirrors, or in assorted low boxes.

Mirrors will be especially effective if the items reflect well. Mirror tiles, available at hardware and lumber supply houses, come in twelve-inch squares, and can be placed on your table in a number of different configurations. Because they have a more finished apperance, tiles with beveled edges are worth the additional cost.

A few small containers of foliage placed among the items in your collection complete the display. The containers can be of different sizes, but all should be small. Short crystal water glasses, ounce-size measuring glasses, or cordials would work well. Very little foliage will be needed. Several small spider plantlets could be effective. Small-leaf ivy, boxwood sprigs, or stems of parsley would all be attractive. Assorted shades of green will provide all the necessary color.

The items of your collection are the featured attraction; flowers would only detract. Small votive candles could be placed in the display in lieu of tall candles. Everything should be low so your guests can talk above it, or even about it.

A collection of early salt dips is accented by a few sprigs of sedum and a clutch of seed heads from a clematis vine.

31

THROUGH A GLASS BOWL CLEARLY

Glass is so beautiful that you should always be able to see through it, and what you see should be clean and sparse. It is a good idea to add a little bleach to the water to keep it fresh.

Even for a round glass bubble bowl such as the one described here, you will need a pinholder to keep the flowers from leaning tiredly against the edge of the bowl. Inexpensive pinholders are frequently available at large multi-department grocery stores or garden centers. Spray the pinholder silver to minimize its appearance.

These glass bowls come in assorted sizes, but for a six-inch one, you will need three 18-inch stems of a blue spiky flower such as stock or delphinium, and three 12-inch stems of a white flower such as carnation, daisy, lily, petunia, or rose.

If you can find them, a sparkling addition to this design would be several loops of clear faceted bead sprays. These are long whips of clear plastic line with beads glued in place four inches apart. You can wind them into loops and then hold the loops in position by tying them together with thread. Use stems of the crystal bead sprays as if they were foliage. If this idea appeals to you, and you cannot find these sprays ready-made, make your own by glueing clear faceted beads along the length of a heavy plastic fishing line using tacky glue or a glue gun. Lay the beaded line down to dry. In your arrangement the beads will sparkle with reflected light and add magic to a special ocassion. A spray or two of delicate foliage such as fern or small-leaf ivy may be added if you feel the arrangment needs it.

When the flowers and foliage are in place, fill the bottom of each bowl with clear glass marbles to hide the pinholder. Shattered glass from a car window will serve the same purpose. Because automotive glass is designed not to cut when it breaks, it will not cut when you handle it, either. Though it is much less attractive, you may be satisfied to cover the pinholder by wrapping it with clear plastic wrap. Add water until the bowl is half filled. For larger glass bowls, use more of everything.

A few short fern fronds are held in place under the glass marbles so they will reflect attractively in the mirror base.

33

WINTER IS ICE AND GLASS

Recently clear glass trees, molded in shapes of spruce or pine, have been appearing in the Christmas decorations section of department and variety stores. They are solid glass and quite heavy. If you place three or more of these glass trees in varying heights on mirrors in the center of the table, they can be the foundation of an elegant centerpiece. If you cannot find them in different sizes, raise two of them to different heights by placing them on clear glass bases, such as overturned ashtrays or candle holders.

The mirrors may be purchased from building supply stores where they are sold as twelve-inch square wall tiles. The mirror tiles with the bevelled edges are worth the extra expense because they give a finished appearance to your centerpiece.

Artificial snow can be added to the scene with the use of small pulled fluffs of aquarium filter material. This product has an attractive glossy appearance which is more attractive than the dull look of cotton batting. Sprinkle the scene with "diamond dust," a product available at most craft stores. The dust will add delightful touches of twinkle. Tiny crystal beads, or pearls from discarded costume jewelry can be scattered across the mirrored tiles and on the aquarium-filter fluffs.

Small glass containers of water, filled with bits of shattered car windows or clear glass marbles to support stems, may hold sprigs of fresh baby's breath if you want to add plant material. The small glass vases could also hold crystal beads on wire stems.

As a final touch, place several clear glass votive candles among the trees and snow banks.

LET THEM FLOAT

The main thing to keep in mind about trying to create a centerpiece of floating flowers is that all flowers do not float. To create an attractive effect with floating flowers, the flowers should be skimming above the surface of the water. Half-submerged flowers with only the tips of their petals showing above the water are not attractive and, further, they do not last when they are waterlogged.

You can experiment to see which flowers do float and are suitable for the bowl you want to use, or you can choose the flowers that appeal to you and make a little raft for each flower. The flower floats could be thin slices of styrofoam, cork, or small cardboard rings dipped in melted wax. Each float should be constructed to allow space for the flower stem, but in no case should the float be visible.

The effect of a floating centerpiece should be light and airy. The water should be seen. A deep container, such as a brandy snifter or fish bowl, would be ideal. You might have an interesting seashell or a small ceramic or glass fish or frog resting on the bottom in the water.

Adding foliage, if any is needed, will not be a problem since almost any leaf will float.

PERMANENT SUMMER CENTERPIECE

It is always reassuring to have an attractive table arrangement constantly available for whenever it might be needed. It could, like mine, occupy the center of your dining room table all summer long or it could be packed away in a box or plastic bag.

For the container use the largest, lowest, prettiest, clear glass bowl you can find. Fill the bottom of the container with clear glass marbles or pieces of shattered car windows.

The flowers needed will be three silk water-lilies and two silk waterlily buds. Because you may want to use the flowers again for an-

other arrangement, coil up the stems as tightly as you can so they will not be seen under the flowers, and place the flowers and buds around the outside edge of the bowl.

Now for the fun! Fill the center of the bowl with some of your favorite pretty things. You may want to use a paperweight, or you might have a few glass fishing floats. Add several interesting sea shells or a piece of crystalized rock. It's your centerpiece. Fill it with the things you think are pretty and eye-catching.

36

A FOUNTAIN OF FOLIAGE

Water and plants, fountains and gardens, there is an easy compatibility. Why not create a fountain of foliage in the center of your table? A lovely low glass bowl will set the scene.

Spray-paint a large pinholder silver, and place it in the bottom of a shallow bowl. Use tall wispy green foliage such as grasses, split yucca leaves, iris, or sanseveria leaves to create a fountain effect springing up from the middle of the bowl. One, two, or three flowers may appear to be coming up through the center of the fountain. The airier the effect, the better.

As a final touch before you add the water, fill the bottom of the bowl with clear glass marbles, or pieces of shattered automobile glass to hide the pinholder. Broken car window glass may be obtained from an automobile glass repair shop, and clear glass marbles can be found at import stores and florist shops. Some people use clear plastic wrap instead of glass to hide the pinholder, but it is not as attractive.

37

The garden lantern shown beside the lady for the photograph would be placed behind her for a centerpiece.

THE LADY IN THE GARDEN

Feature a favorite figurine in your next centerpiece display. Only a few tall leaves will be needed to accent your figure and it will be fun for you to experiment with the ancient Japanese art of sand painting.

The base for the centerpiece should be a black-lacquered board. Such bases are standard equipment for Japanese flower arrangers. If you do not have a suitable black-lacquered board, improvise with a tray.

Next you will need two ceramic or porcelain figures, or one figure and another smaller complimentary porcelain object such as a lamp or an animal figure. Behind the main figure place a cup pinholder, preferably a small half-circle type if you have it. Into the cup pinholder place three cyperus (papyrus) stems. If the umbrella-like leaves are too large, trim them. Any leaf that will give the effect of an umbrella over the figures will be appropriate. Add a bit of additional low foliage behind the figure to soften the effect.

Then, because this is a centerpiece to be seen from all sides, add the second figure on the opposite side.

To integrate the picture you are creating and to add reality to the scene, create a pathway on each side by lightly sprinkling very fine white sand on the lacquer base. Sugar would be a reasonable substitute for the sand. Using a feather, lightly spread the sand into a flowing trail.

For an additonal naturalistic touch, you can put a few tiny perlite "stones" in the sand near the figures.

CREATE A WATER SCENE

There is a wonderful style of Japanese flower arranging called Moribana which frequently makes water an element of the design. For this kind of arrangement a long container and two pinholders, one larger than the other, will be needed.

Mentally divide the container into quarters, and place both pinholders in the same quarter. Two groups of plant material should then be created, one at least four times larger and taller than the other.

The two arrangements must be complementary and vertical rather than spreading. Tall, wispy branches of barely emerging foliage are good to use. Begin by covering the pinholders with a small tightly-leafed foliage such as parsley. The smaller pinholder should contain material which looks as if it is growing under the taller material, just as it appears in nature. Keep the arrangements simple and sparse and the water clean. A few special stones might be placed in the water, if you like. Make it peaceful.

ONLY THREE FLOWERS FOR EACH TABLE

The secret of this centerpiece rests with the base, a gold-lacquered Oriental tray of a kind available from any inexpensive import store. However, any simple dish or plastic tray can be used, if it is sprayed with gold floral spray. The container is a tuna can spray-painted bright gold. Fill the can with dampened floral foam.

Each arrangement will need four to seven stems of foliage, all of the same variety, in lengths from three to twelve inches. When placing the foliage in the foam, aim for a layered effect, as if the leaves were growing out of the can. The lowest leaves should cover the edges of the container. You might use geraniumn leaves, galax, grape leaves, even hosta.

When the foliage is in place, simply insert three large flowers, such as purple Dutch iris, at different heights and facing in different directions.

A pink flowering Kalanchoe, removed from its growing
pot, is nestled temporarily in a bed of green cellophane
Easter grass inside an Oriental bowl on a stand.

42

USE YOUR HOUSE PLANTS

Any house plant of appropriate size in good condition with healthy leaves and a good symmetrical shape can be set into a pretty pot and placed in the center of the table for a centerpiece. A brass or copper pot would be handsome. Do not hesitate to trim a plant to improve its shape. If the sight of dirt is distasteful, a little bright green cellophane Easter grass, Spanish or sphagnum moss, or excelsior may be spread over the surface. Grass or moss may be stored in a plastic bag and re-used.

Buy a few flowers, whichever are the least expensive, and stick the stems right into the dirt of your favorite potted plant. You will be surprised how many people will ask, "What kind of plant is that?"

A few of the many plants that would be good for this kind of centerpiece are pothos, ferns, and ivy. Baby's tears is perfect—flowers will look as if they are growing right out of the plant. Remember to keep turning your plants so light doesn't always hit them from the same side and cause irregular growth.

And if you don't have a lovely pot to slip the house plant into? Knock the plant right out of its growing pot, wrap it in clear plastic wrap, put a rubber band around it, and put it in a bowl. If the bowl is too deep, put some soft padding in the bottom—wadded paper or foam packing "peanuts" are good for this—and set the plant on top. Spread moss or Easter grass over the surface of the plant. Afterwards unwrap the plant and set it right back into its growing pot.

If you can find a wire egg basket, the kind that is shaped like a chicken, fill it with cellophane Easter grass and put a plant inside.

Because the basket is so large and the plants used are so small, this centerpiece holds six assorted foliage plants with a few white chrysanthemums inserted in the floral foam between the pots.

GRADUATION CELEBRATION

Graduation celebrations, coming as they usually do in warm weather, are frequently held out-of-doors. What could be more appropriate than a large basketful of plant material for the centerpiece? If desired, colorful ribbons in school colors can be wound around the handle of the basket. Simply secure the ends of one or more ribbons by tucking them into the weavers at the base of the handle. Wind the ribbons tightly around the handle and secure the other ends in the same way. The ribbon will stay in place.

Protect the basket from moisture by lining it with either aluminum or plastic wrap. Then put three, 3-inch pots of houseplants in the basket. Variegated dracena or diffenbachia would work well. Each plant should be about eighteen inches tall.

Between the pots place pieces of dampened floral foam and insert stems of cut flowers into the foam. Lilies would be gorgeous, but outrageously expensive. Daisies, chrysanthemums, carnations, or garden flowers in the colors of your choice would be the most reasonable and durable choices. Add foliage with the flowers to help cover the foam. Remember that both flowers and foliage should be conditioned in deep water for at least an hour before they are used in any arrangement.

A light, airy touch can be added by inserting small bunches of ornamental grasses wired together into sprays.

A large bow to match the ribbon on the handle can be wired to the basket or inserted into the foliage. Place an object with some special meaning for the graduate near the basket.

A BASKET OF SPRING

For a simple springtime centerpiece, fill a basket with a blooming plant. Depending upon the size of the basket, one or more potted plants may also be placed inside. Cover the surface of the plants with moss, Easter grass, or excelsior. Let the grass fall gracefully over the edge of the basket. If your arrangement is for Easter, a few dyed eggs or jelly beans can be added to the grass.

The same arrangement can be made by burying a jar of water containing a few flowers and foliage inside some Easter grass in a basket.

A SMALL GIFT

Taking small flower arrangements to friends when you visit for special occasions is coming more and more into vogue as the cost of flower delivery soars. With this kind of flower arrangement, the container becomes part of the gift so it is a good idea to collect an assortment of suitable containers before they are needed. Garage sales and flea markets are a good source of interesting little containers. Odd cordial glasses, cut glass toothpick holders, and shot glasses are ideal. Variety stores and florist shops, also, often have attractive, but inexpensive, small containers.

For height in a flower design in a small container, use tiny twisted bare branches. Add a few ivy or African violet leaves, or a tiny sprig of fern. All you will need from the florist is a small stem of baby's breath and several small flowers from a flower spray. You could use an African violet or two from your own houseplant, or a tiny silk flower from a spray of artificial flowers you have on hand. Small flowers from your garden could be dried and stored for use in this kind of miniature arrangement.

A GIFT FROM THE SEA

Find a shell that will sit flat and fill it with water. Then stuff the inside of the shell with cotton so the water will not run out. Fill the opening with a small piece of dampened floral foam.

Place three lengths of vine tendrils, eight, five, and three inches long, to the back, side and front of the design. Add a few sprigs of small-leafed foliage such as boxwood, parsley, or herbs. Two or three miniature flowers or buds will complete the arrangement. Soak the flowers completely in deep water for at least an hour before you use them.

MAKE THEM AHEAD

You might like to make several small silk flower arrangements and store them in plastic bags until you need them. A one and one half-inch colorful pottery container with a small opening will hold a delightful carry-out arrangement of silk flowers. You may have to trim heavy wire stems to make them fit into the container opening.

First insert a three-inch vine tendril or tiny bare branch of some kind into the container for height. Because this will be such a tiny arrangement, take apart a spray of silk flowers and use small leaves and flowers separately. You will need about three of each.

An arrangement of this kind can also be placed in a large wooden bead with a small square of cardboard glued to the bottom to keep it from rolling. The plastic caps from used spray perfume bottles also make useful containers for miniature arrangements.

Grass seed heads, both real and artificial, make an interesting addition to the real twigs and the artificial flowers.

A CENTERPIECE OF SILK AND DRIED MATERIALS

For the base of this centerpiece, choose an irregular slice of wood that will match the feeling of the dried grasses.

In the center of the base, place a cup pinholder. Put a piece of nylon stocking over the needles and push a small block of styrofoam over the nylon. This will enable you to remove the styrofoam later without creating a messy clean-up job in the pinholder. The metal cup holder will be heavy enough to support the weight of your arrangement.

First, cover the styrofoam with several short pieces of small-leaved silk fern. Keep it very low.

Next add the main attraction of this arrangement, two realistic-looking silk orchids. One should be about nine inches tall and the other, seven inches.

Fill in with either artificial or real dried grasses with their seed heads, which should be of different lengths. Under the orchids and grasses, add a few short silk flowers. Make it appear as if they are growing there. On the side that does not have an orchid, make the flowers taller. You may also add an interesting piece of wood or a dried pod on this side.

Scatter a few loose Sweet Gum balls, acorns, or pinecones around the base and even, perhaps, one caught in the grasses. Try to make it look as if the whole centerpiece were growing up out of the dried materials of winter.

Because this design contains no fresh material it can be used and re-used as the need arises. To retire this centerpiece temporarily, cover it with a plastic bag and remove it to a closet for a rest.

*Did you guess that the large exotic flowers are real
dahlias and the small filler flowers are silk?*

SILK FLOWERS FOR APARTMENT DWELLERS

If you live in an apartment, you should keep on hand about ten really fine silk flowers. They should be the kind of silk flowers that look real, and they should be in colors suitable for your rooms.

Silk flowers can be inserted right into the dirt in a potted house plant. The houseplant and its growing pot can then be set inside a decorative ceramic or metal container, or a basket, and used as a centerpiece. If you object to seeing the soil, the top of the container can be covered with cellophane grass, moss, or excelsior.

Arrangements of all-silk flowers and foliage are made by inserting their wire stems into styrofoam. If real foliage is used in an arrangement with silk flowers, green floral foam that holds water will be needed. To use silk flowers with a pinholder, slip the wire stem of the silk flower into a tube of some kind—hollow stems of grass, bamboo, pampas grass, even a length of plastic straw. The tube will stick into the pinholder.

Silk flowers may also serve for those occasions when you are making a centerpiece of real flowers, and you find you need just a few more flowers. It will be hard to discern the few silk flowers among the real ones.

To clean silk flowers or foliage, just swish them over a jet of steam from a tea kettle.

Long vegetables such as egg plant, yellow squash, carrots, and corn are useful at the ends with the grasses, while the round material such as peppers, apples, patty pan squash, plums, and pears snuggle into the side.

THANKSGIVING

Thanksgiving means harvest and plenty, decoratively speaking, and is the perfect time for a centerpiece expressing abundancy. Your arrangement should be long and lush and bursting with fruit, vegetables, grasses (to represent grain), and, if you have one, a decoy.

Choose a long tray, board, or bowl and place a brick of styrofoam in the center to fill space that will not show and to provide a backdrop to keep things from rolling. If you have a decoy, place that on top of the styrofoam. If not, select several of the largest fruit or vegetables for the top spot—a pineapple, a long squash or gourd, two eggplants.

Begin placing the other fruit and vegetables around until you are satisfied with the appearance of your arrangement. There should be a sense of overall balance. Grapes should be divided to provide similar bunches for each side. Oranges are troublesome because they roll. If necessary, fruit and vegetables can be held in place with toothpicks. Good choices include pears, peppers, green and red apples, squash, scrubbed carrots, ears of corn, and small eggplants. Try to avoid onions and cabbage-family vegetables because of their undesirable odors. Walnuts, mushrooms, kumquats, and lady apples are good for filling spaces.

Grasses with seed heads that look like grain can be tied into bunches and placed at each end to provide length. Sprigs of foliage can be used to fill spaces, as can short bunches of tied grass. If the sprays of foliage will not stay in place, wire them to a florist pick or popsicle stick and insert the stick into an open space between vegetables.

CHRISTMAS HOLLY AND LIGHTS

The quickest and easiest way to create a last minute Christmas centerpiece is by laying holly sprigs in the center of the table. Take care to hide the cut ends of the holly stems under the leaves of another branch. Whether you are buying the holly or cutting your own, choose branches that will lie as flat as possible on your table. Branches with a lot of curves will have to be cut or broken to make them co-operate. Move the pieces of holly around until you like the look of it. Holly will not stay fresh-looking for a very long time out of water, but spraying the branches with a dessicant will extend their decorative life.

Place lots of candles among the holly. In fact, it may be easier to place the candlesticks first, then spread the holly. The holders need not match, but they should be alike—all silver, all brass, all glass, all votive. Add some shiny red balls to pick up the twinkle of the candle light. There is nothing more inviting than to step into a house that is aglow with candles during the holidays.

CREATE A CHRISTMAS SCENE

If you are a dollhouse owner, or a miniature railroad enthusiast, Christmas can be a good time to put your hobby on display for everyone to enjoy. Using pieces from your collection, create a small scene to sit in a circle of greens in the middle of the table. It could be as simple as a table, rug, and chair with a Santa figure, or it could become a miniature wonderland up to, and including, such details as small tools, tiny table settings, or Lilliputian figures.

Whether the scene is to represent indoors or out-of-doors, a small Christmas tree with tiny beads, which have been removed from discarded costume jewelry and glued into the branches, will add a seasonal touch. In an indoors scene, you could surround the tree with tiny gifts.

Around your vignette place a circle of greens. If the composition is small enough, it might fit inside a ready-made wreath. Remember to make your scene attractive from all sides. Place candlesticks on the table outside the greens.

Though only the white satin rose buds and dried baby's breath are visible in the photograph, chains of tiny silver beads and dozens of small silver balls also hang in the branches of this rather formal Christmas centerpiece.

A CHRISTMAS TREE CENTERPIECE

At Christmas time, small plastic trees, fifteen to eighteen inches tall, can often be found in stores that deal in seasonal merchandise. Frequently these inexpensive trees come pressed flat in clear plastic bags and will have to be manipulated a bit to bring them to their fullest appearance. Each tree is usually supplied with an ugly plastic stand that should be discarded or else an apron of some kind will have to be made to cover it.

Ideally the tree should be imbedded in a pot or bowl of plaster, and the surface of the plaster spread with dried moss or artificial sprigs of foliage. However, if using plaster seems too messy a project, push the tree, with glue smeared on its trunk, down on a brick of styrofoam which has been fixed into an attractive container.

To enhance the appearance of the little tree, first spray it lightly with powder blue floral paint. You should still be able to see green through the paint. Then spray it again with a light misting of white floral paint. The tree will look one hundred percent better—very like a blue spruce.

Decorate your tree with tiny tree balls, small ribbon bows, miniature birds or fruit. Add some sparkle to the decorations by using old costume jewelry. Earrings can be clipped right onto the branches. Strings of beads can be used as if they were chains, or taken apart, and each bead wired into place separately. Interesting jewelry can be found at flea markets and white elephant tables.

An all white tree could be made by spraying the tree white and decorating it with white ribbon, pearls and crystal beads.

Hand crafted decorations seem especially appropriate for the Holidays.

MAKE YOUR OWN CHRISTMAS CANDLE

To make your own Christmas candle, all you need is two or more packages of paraffin wax from the grocery store and a length of wicking from a craft store. Wick size is determined by the width of the candle being produced; so, if you have a choice, get the size for candles three inches or wider.

Paraffin comes as four slabs in a one pound box. Place a length of wicking between the two center slabs. Then, using a little melted wax from an old candle as "glue," stick all four slabs together. If you prefer a taller candle, fix another set of four slabs on the top of the first set, sticking them all together with more "glue," being careful to run the wick through both sets of slabs, top to bottom.

Next, melt an additional pound of wax (two pounds for the taller candle) by heating it in one container placed inside a larger container of boiling water. An old sauce pan or any container with a handle is best to hold the wax. Wax is HIGHLY FLAMMABLE so never place it directly over a heat source. As soon as the wax is melted, remove it from the heat and stir it vigorously with a spoon until it becomes frothy. Dab the frothy wax over the slabs of parrafin with the spoon, covering the paraffin completely.

If desired, colorful sequins, stars, or glitter may be sprinkled over the outside while the wax is still soft.

Tie a ribbon around the candle and set it on a bed of greens to which tiny glass balls or natural berries may be added. The candle would look equally well standing inside a wreath in the middle of your table. Be sure you have some sort of protection such as a tray, place mat, or clear plastic wrap between the candle and a fine table surface or table cloth.

To make a round snowball candle, fill both halves of a cleaned-out grapefruit rind with melted paraffin. Let the wax cool and harden, then remove it from the grapefruit rinds by pushing up from the bottom to pop it out. Place a wick between the halves, "glue" them together, and cover with a coat of frothy wax, as described above.

When they are completed, these glittering tree decorations have a crystal crust reminiscent of sugar plums.

A BOWL OF CHRISTMAS BALLS

Colorful and glittery Christmas tree balls are fun to make alone or in group workshops. Placed in a bowl with a few sprigs of evergreen they make an attractive centerpiece at home or for a fund raising luncheon. Offer them for sale as part of the fund raising effort and they will sell quickly!

Buy medium-size styrofoam balls and green pipe cleaners. Assemble swatches of small--patterned Christmas material, lace, ribbons, sequins, and colorful marking pens. From a craft store purchase decoupage sealer/glue called Mod Podge, and small-particle glitter called "diamond dust," or "Mother-of-pearl dust."

The fun begins. To make a hanger for the ball, punch a hole in the styrofoam with an ice pick, smear some craft glue over a three inch piece of pipe cleaner, and push it into the hole. Bend the pipe cleaner to form a hook. Glue small pieces of material in colorful Christmas patterns over the surface of the ball. Add bits of lace or ribbon, if you like. Draw swirls, circles, or blobs of color over the surface with marking pens, or make the ball a single bright color.

When the ball has been decorated to your satisfaction, paint the surface of the ball heavily with decoupage lacquer and hang it to dry over a string stretched across your newspaper-covered work surface. The lacquer looks milky as it is applied, but it dries clear. When the surface is dry, apply a second coat of lacquer and sprinkle it with glitter dust while it is still wet.

The stainless steel egg holder displays each egg individually to show the many ways they can be decorated.

TRY THESE FANCY EASTER EGGS

Wonderfully cheerful and imaginatively contrived Easter eggs can be made with styrofoam eggs, a few pieces of small-patterned material swatches, and a special water-base glue and sealer called Mod Podge.

First, small pieces of patterned material are cut out and glued onto the outside of a styrofoam egg with white craft glue. Choose small flowers or stripes that seem compatible with the size of the styrofoam egg. The styrofoam can be completely covered with material or small designs may be glued onto the egg in only two or three places. After you have completed your first egg, you will see how easy this craft is and how many variations are possible with the designs. You can use lace or ribbons, you can draw designs on the eggs with marking pens in various colors, or you can draw swirls of colors over the material. Let your imagination run riot.

When the design is in place, stick three tooth picks into the egg to form a set of supporting legs, and have a block of styrofoam ready to support the toothpick legs. Then, using a paint brush, generously coat the entire surface of the egg with Mod Podge. It looks milky when it goes on, but it dries clear. A second coat will be needed after the first coat dries.

Also available at craft stores is a product called diamond dust—tiny specks of glittery material. Mother-of-pearl dust is also available in different colors. Sprinkle one of these over the last coat of sealer. Remove the toothpick legs.

The eggs are gay and cheerful as they are, or they can be embellished with ribbons and tiny flowers. To tie a ribbon around an egg, run a thin line of glue along the surface and lay the ribbon on top of the glue.

A basket of finished eggs next to a stuffed rabbit in the center of your table makes a cheerful Easter centerpiece. These eggs also make attractive gifts for friends at this time of the year.

THE WEDDING REHEARSAL DINNER

For an occasion as special as a wedding rehearsal dinner, it is fun to personalize the event by determining what the couple's special interests are and featuring them in your theme.

If *she* thinks frogs are cute, use a ceramic frog or two. If *he* likes baseball, cluster some balls together in a bowl and add a rolled program from a game. If the bride and groom have a shared interest, so much the better. Are they birdwatchers? Look for an interesting bird figure to place in your design. For hikers, use minerals or interesting rocks. If they enjoy fishing, do a water arrangement with a few flowers and foliage, then place a ceramic fish or two in the water. Ceramic figures of all kinds can be found in variety and import stores, or at garage sales and flea markets.

Once the featured objects are chosen, make them the main attraction. Objects can be raised on wooden blocks with some foliage spread around to conceal the blocks. If flowers are added, keep them small. The personalized objects should be the center of attention.

If it is impossible to pinpoint an appropriate symbol, feature their favorite color, or contrive a design conveying the astrological signs of the bridal couple.

POINSETTIAS FOR A WINTER WEDDING

A lovely flower frequently thought of as a Christmas flower but fortunately available for most of the winter is the vibrant, long-lasting, multi-colored poinsettia. These beautiful plants are available from November through February, especially if you make arrangments in advance to have them for a particular date.

Poinsettia plants today come in a large range of varieties, sizes, and colors and are entirely appropriate just as they are for use as a centerpiece. Each plant should be set into a larger brass-finished metal pot. The plant can be raised, if necessary, by placing pebbles in the bottom of the container. Fill the area between the plant and the container with pieces of wet floral foam, and place sprigs of evergreen in the foam to hide the soil, soften the edge of the container, and fill out the spindly poinsettia foliage.

Two brass candlesticks with candles to match the color of the flowers will complete the centepiece for each table. For a head, or bridal table, simply use a larger plant in a larger brass container.

Poinsettias are available in white, pink, several shades of red, and in a choice of variegation. All are appealing, but the white ones might be especially memorable for a winter wedding. Poinsettia flowers can also be made into lovely bouquets.

These little bouquets, that are so quick and easy to make, would create magic for any occasion.

WHEN THE WEDDING RECEPTION TABLES ARE LONG AND NARROW

Wedding receptions held in church social halls and other large reception rooms often must be arranged to accomodate many long, narrow tables not suitable for one single centerpiece. For this situation, lengths of ribbon can be looped down the length of each table and small bouquets of flowers placed along the length. The ribbon should be laid in gentle turns and graceful waves.

The flowers for the bouquets can be cut from the garden, purchased from a florist, or be a combination of both. Condition the flowers carefully by placing them, immediatley after cutting (or re-cut them freshly when you bring them from the florist), in deep water for several hours. Plan to make enough bouquets so they can be placed every three feet along the length of each table. Five to seven flowers and five to seven stems of foliage will be needed for each bouquet.

To make each bouquet, gather a few flowers and several stems of foliage in your hand moving them about until they look just right. Put a rubber band tightly around each bouquet to keep it as you arranged it, and trim the stems evenly across the bottom so they are not more than three or four inches long. Stand the bouquets in water until a few hours before the reception. At that time, wrap the stems with green floral tape that is sticky on both sides. Wrap ribbon over the tape, making a bow for each bouquet with eight-inch streamers. Bundled like this and misted lighty just before they go on the tables, these little bouquets will hold up for the length of the party.

Small to medium size flowers should be used. The ones that will stay fresh the longest are chrysanthemums, daisies, statice, baby's breath, and any flower from a bulb. Good foliage to use would be ivy, fern, boxwood, columbine, or azalea.

A similar, but larger, bouquet may be made to rest on the cake table. It, too, should have ribbon streamers.

LET THE GOOD LUCK RICE BE YOUR CENTERPIECE

Here is another way to solve the problem of decorating long, narrow tables at a wedding reception. This arrangement has the additional advantage of not needing to be done at the last minute. These little table decorations can be made up weeks in advance of the occasion and quickly placed on the tables, one at each person's place, whenever it is most convenient to do so.

Buy enough white tulle, marquisette, or similar delicate fabric to provide an eight-inch square of material for each person who will be present. Into the center of each square of fabric, pour a little pile of rice or birdseed and tie the material together with a length of ribbon in a color suitable to the occasion. Please do consider using birdseed, however, because rice is difficult to remove from sidewalks and driveways. Rice also poses a hazard for certain kinds of birds who may die as the result of eating it.

If you prefer, instead of white, use colored material with contrasting ribbon to make the little bundles. Cut the ribbon so there will be streamers which are a little longer than the height of the bag of grain.

In the center of the ribbon on each sack, poke a silk flower or two. Long stems will not be necessary, so you can purchase artificial flowers that come as sprays with more than one flower to a stem and cut them apart. Be sure to use all of the artificial foliage that comes with the flowers.

Alternative possibilities for these small arrangements include using real flowers and foliage that have been well conditioned the day before; or adding real foliage to a few artificial flowers, and enhancing the overall table design by twining a length of the same ribbon used to tie the bundles down the middle of the length of the table.

Later, when the reception is drawing to a close, the little bags can be opened and the contents thrown at the happy couple as they leave to start their new life together.

Sometimes simple can be dramatic.

WINE BOTTLES A GO-GO

Wine bottles should be very easy to accumulate in quantity. Ask any restaurant to save you a boxful! Perhaps you can get some pretty little individual-serving wine bottles from a stewardess during your next airplane flight. Gather plenty of bottles, though, because you will need at least three bottles on each table. One bottle would look awfully lonely as a centerpiece.

All the bottles on a single table should be the same color. They might be different shades of the same color, but white, brown and green wine bottles together would not be as attractive as several of the same color. Select a variety of sizes, however, to add interest.

Each wine bottle will need one tall stem of foliage, which should extend above the bottle at least the same height as the bottle itself. Use a mixture of foliages on the same table, if you like. Then, put three flowers in the largest bottle, two flowers in the middle size bottle, and one in the smallest bottle. If the flower stems are not long enough for the flowers to look graceful, stick a length of wire up into the stems. Only the bottom of a flower's stem needs to be in water, but you should avoid resting a flower head right down on the neck of the bottle.

Carnations in mixed colors would be handsome in the large bottles with mini-carnations for the small bottles.

73

Wild golden rod and bachelor buttons gathered from an empty city lot work very well in a plain brown paper wrapper. A simple gathering of foliage would be effective in a more colorful bag.

74

PAPER BAG CONTAINERS

Paper bags are so versatile! You can scallop them, you can cut holes in them, you can cuff them. You can cut them short, you can leave them long, you can paint them with crayons, magic markers or acrylic paint. You can use one large bag or three small bags for each table and anywhere from five to nine bags for a head table. Inside each bag will be a can or jar of water, but they don't have to be alike because they won't show.

The bag itself will help support the plant material, so you won't need anything in the inside jars but water. To get a large effect from a few flowers, use a mass of foliage with only three or five flowers in each centerpiece and tie brightly colored yarn around the bag just above the container.

Colorful yarn trim will make an even greater contribution if, instead of fresh garden flowers and foliage, you use bunches of dried roadside flowers and grasses.

Paper bags, especially white ones, can also be used as luminaries when interesting patterns are cut out or hole-punched in them. To create the same pattern on both sides with a single cut, take a lunch-sized bag, folded flat, and fold it again longwise. Working with the folded edge, cut half of the shape you want and a whole shape will be cut in both sides. The cut outs will be more effective if they are small. Hole punches are useful for creating patterns of holes. To turn a paper bag into a luminary, fill the bottom with sand or pebbles and put a candle inside.

Only three hydrangea flowers are needed for this centerpiece. Because these flowers do not have the stately stems of daffodils, some foliage is also included.

FLOWERS AND RECORDS FOR A MUSICAL OCCASION

This design is guaranteed not to be good for the records, so collect old, unwanted 78's or 45's, or buy them at a garage sale. Get at least three records for the center of each table. Medium size food cans will serve as containers. Make sure you have at least two alike for each table because you will be stacking one on top of another to create pillar containers. The can on the bottom may be turned upside down. Tape the cans together around the rims in the middle, then spray-paint them flat black.

Five daffodils, or any other flowers of comparable size with handsome stems, will be needed for each table. Because daffodils look best with their long stems showing, pack wads of damp newspaper into the bottom half of each top can. Then, holding five long-stemmed daffodils, with a few of their own leaves, in one hand, arrange them so they are all facing different directions at slightly different heights. When you have them the way you like them, trim off the stems so they are even and, holding them in the can with one hand, stuff more wads of damp newspaper around them to hold them upright. Fill the cans with water and cover the top of the newspaper with low foliage.

Of course, the flowers will have been conditioned by being placed in water for at least an hour before being arranged. If, instead of fresh flowers, dried grasses, leaves, and flowers are used, simply gather them together in your hand, trim them, wrap a thread around them at the bottom, and fix them in the can in the same way.

77

A photograph, such as this one cut from a popular fashion magazine, is ideal for a fund-raising fashion show luncheon.

GET SOME HELP FROM THE MAGAZINES

Your assignment? Create centerpieces for twelve large round tables for the local fund raiser. Budget? Zip. Why not use cut-out magazine pictures, pasted on posterboard tents, standing in the center of each table with a bouquet of foliage to one side?

Look for full-page color illustrations from the magazines. Choose the biggest, brightest, lightest pictures you can find and the ones most appropriate to the occasion. Or, try clippings from the school newspaper, covers from the church bulletin, pictures of flowers from garden catalogs, left-over invitations or notices of the event itself. If you use photographs, or anything that you want to recover later, make sure you fix the pictures to the backing with rubber cement. Whatever you use, you will need two pictures for each table, one for each side of the cardboard sandwich board.

To unify the appearance of the room, the posterboard backing should be the same size and color for each table, as should the containers for the plant material.

Make the cardboard tents stand upright by taping the posterboard backings together, head to head, on the inside (the side without the pictures) then flipping them over so the tape doesn't show.

On one side of each tent, place a small arrangement of foliage. Tuna fish cans, spray-painted the same color as the posterboard and filled with dampened floral foam, can hold assorted foliage. Arrange the greens so the tallest stem is in the center and all other stems are progressively shorter. Make sure the edges of the cans are covered with foliage. Garden foliage particularly will need to be immersed in cold water for at least an hour, and preferably overnight, before it is used.

THE OLD FAN IN THE CLAY POT TRICK

Inexpensive import stores are popping up everywhere and what treasures they hold for party centerpieces! Take, for instance, the round, rigid palm-leaf fans of the kind associated with rocking chairs on front porches before the days of air conditioning. These grand old fans are handsome and inexpensive. Formerly available only in tan, they now come in many vivid colors, which makes them look like huge overblown flowers. And, they have two good sides!

All that remains to fill a room with cheerful centerpieces is a gathering of flower pots and a bag full of garden foliage.

Stuff dampened green floral foam into each pot and push the handle of a fan into the center. Fill in around the base of the fan with short sprigs of fresh foliage. You might tie a bow with ribbon streamers around the bottom of the fan if you need more color. If the tables are large, use a woven straw mat as a base under the clay pot to enlarge the effect of each centerpiece.

Done!

BASKETS AND BOWS

If you can locate enough inexpensive four-inch round baskets for a roomful of arrangements, the rest is easy. One basket will decorate each table. Because no fresh plant material is used, these arrangements can be made well in advance.

Cut a piece of brown floral foam for each basket. This product is designed for use with dried and silk arrangments. Into the foam insert stems of dried baby's breath which is available reasonably from the florist. The baby's breath should be about eight to ten inches high and fluff out over the edges of the basket.

Next, tie bows of half-inch wide florist ribbon in assorted pastel colors. You will need at least nine bows for each centerpiece. Wire the bows onto the blunt end of a six-inch bamboo shish-ke-bob stick, using fine florist wire. Bamboo sticks are available in Oriental food stores and, frequently, in gourmet food departments.

Poke the be-ribboned sticks into the plastic foam among the baby's breath. The sticks will not be seen because they are the same color as the dried material.

This design would also make a thoughtful shut-in gift.
Deliver it in a clear plastic bag tied with a ribbon.

FOR A CARD PARTY

These centerpieces are suitable for small tables of four to six people and, though originally planned for a Valentine's Day event, they would work equally well for any winter card party. Centerpieces like this can be made well in advance of party day, and they make excellent table prizes.

The container is a four-inch square berry basket. All the baskets should be alike. If you can find inexpensive enameled ones, buy them. Line the baskets with pretty pieces of calico. Then put a small piece of styrofoam inside to hold the plant material. Fern pins (that look a little like hair pins) may be used to secure the styrofoam. Push the pins up from the bottom into the styrofoam.

Stems of dried baby's breath, about eight to ten inches tall, should be pushed into the styrofoam. You will also need seven to nine stems of very small pink and white silk flowers for each basket. Small flowers that are cut from larger sprays of artificial flowers should be the right size. The flower stems should be pushed into the styrofoam through the ba-by's breath. Add three sprays of small artificial pink berries for interest. If you cannot find the right color berries, use floral spray-paint in pink to color whatever berries you are able to find. Spray the paint more heavily on the lowest berries and the ones closest to the stems, because lower and older berries are darker in nature.

When the container is the feature, the plant material can be minimal.

MAKE IT BIG WITH YARN-WRAPPED CANS

It is the impact of color that fills the eye when you enter a room. The larger the room, the more color that will be needed. Here is a suggestion for inexpensive centerpieces for a many-tabled event held in a large room when the budget for decorating is limited.

Collect empty food cans, at least three for each table. The cans should be different sizes and shapes. Next collect an assortment of left-over yarn. Everyone who knits, weaves, or needlepoints has left-over yarn. Spray-paint the cans in a muted or background color such as green. Wrap the cans with yarn, using small dabs of white craft glue where needed to hold the yarn in place. You can form bands of color. You can criss-cross the colors. You can create complicated Indian patterns. Anything goes.

These brightly decorated containers will be the attraction. Plain foliage or dried grasses will be all you need in the cans. A few flowers may be added if you have them, but they are not necessary. Place three cans on each table and, if a larger effect seems called for, sprinkle dried leaves, pine cones, nuts, seashells, or pebbles on the table around the cans. Avoid spreading fresh leaves which will wither quickly, except for succulents such as hens and chicken. All colors and materials should be compatible.

A TABLE OF SUGGESTIONS FOR INEXPENSIVE CENTERPIECE DESIGNS

Here is a table of mix-and-match centerpiece ideas for multi-table occasions. All materials suggested are generally available and reasonably priced.

The most important thing when creating centerpieces for special occasions is—THINK AHEAD! Plan the centerpiece designs based on the season, the meaning of the event, and the budget. Make up a sample arrangement to be sure your idea will work and be attractive. Then line up a work committee and gather the materials you will need. If you are called upon often to do centerpieces, you will always need to be on the lookout for inexpensive items available in large numbers. Seasonal close-out sales, bargain tables, budget import houses, and flea markets can be the source of many usable objects, if you keep your eyes and mind open.

Categories included in the table are bases, containers, mechanics, foliage, features, and flowers.

<u>BASES</u>
trays
place mats
woven straw mats
pieces of sliced wood
handkerchiefs
scarfs
books
records
magazines
building tiles
  floor
  ceramic
  mirror
  metal
swirls of ribbon
scattered beans, buttons
  leaves, pine shavings,
  shells, cones, pods
  fishing floats, marbles
  pebbles, beads, etc.